PLACE VALUE

Penny Dowdy

Crabtree Publishing Company

www.crabtreebooks.com

Author: Penny Dowdy
Coordinating editor: Chester Fisher
Series editor: Jessica Cohn
Editors: Reagan Miller, Molly Aloian
Proofreader: Crystal Sikkens
Project coordinator: Robert Walker
Production coordinator: Margaret Amy Salter
Prepress technician: Margaret Amy Salter
Logo design: Samantha Crabtree
Cover design: Ranjan Singh (Q2AMEDIA)
Design: Neha Gupta (Q2AMEDIA)
Project manager: Santosh Vasudeva (Q2AMEDIA)
Art direction: Rahul Dhiman (Q2AMEDIA)
Photo research: Sejal Sehgal

Photographs:
Adobe Image Library: p. 13
Bigstockphoto: Freerk Brouwer: p. 1 (inset), 6
Corbis: Martin Harvey; Gallo Images: p. 17 (top);
    Farrell Grehan: p. 17 (bottom)
Dreamstime: Slavka: p. 8
Fotolia: Monika Adamczyk: p. 4; Marjory Duc: p. 5; Galem: p. 19 (top)
Istockphoto: Kent Weakley: p. 1, 7
Shutterstock: Galyna Andrushko/Stephen Lynch: p. 11; Cre8tive
    Images: p. 12 (ants); Gravicapa: p. 9; Jeff Gynane: p. 21 (top);
    Tischenko Irina: p. 19 (bottom); Eric Isselée: p. 15, 21 (bottom);
    Scott Leman: cover (insert); Maga: p. 12 (leaves); Nikita Rogul:
    cover; Tawei Wan: p. 21 (middle)

Library and Archives Canada Cataloguing in Publication

Dowdy, Penny
    Place value / Penny Dowdy.

(My path to math)
Includes index.
ISBN 978-0-7787-4343-9 (bound).--ISBN 978-0-7787-4361-3 (pbk)

    1. Place value (Mathematics)--Juvenile literature. 2. Counting--
Juvenile literature. 3. Numeration--Juvenile literature. I. Title.
II. Series: Dowdy, Penny. My path to math.

QA141.3.D69 2008   j513   C2008-906082-2

Library of Congress Cataloging-in-Publication Data

Dowdy, Penny.
    Place value / Penny Dowdy.
       p. cm. -- (My path to math)
    Includes index.
    ISBN-13: 978-0-7787-4361-3 (pbk. : alk. paper)
    ISBN-10: 0-7787-4361-6 (pbk. : alk. paper)
    ISBN-13: 978-0-7787-4343-9 (reinforced library binding : alk. paper)
    ISBN-10: 0-7787-4343-8 (reinforced library binding : alk. paper)
    1. Place value (Mathematics)--Juvenile literature. 2. Counting--Juvenile
literature. 3. Numeracy--Juvenile literature. I. Title. II. Series.

    QA141.3.D645 2008
    513.5--dc22
                                    2008040140

Crabtree Publishing Company

www.crabtreebooks.com   1-800-387-7650

Published in Canada
Crabtree Publishing
616 Welland Ave.
St. Catharines, Ontario
L2M 5V6

Published in the United States
Crabtree Publishing
PMB16A
350 Fifth Ave., Suite 3308
New York, NY 10118

Published in the United Kingdom
Crabtree Publishing
White Cross Mills
High Town, Lancaster
LA1 4XS

Published in Australia
Crabtree Publishing
386 Mt. Alexander Rd.
Ascot Vale (Melbourne)
VIC 3032

Contents

Counting

Can you count? When you count, you use numbers. You start with 1. Then you name the numbers in order. You stop when you run out of things to count!

Activity Box

Find five of something in your room.
Write the figure. Write the word.

How many bees do you see?
1—2—3—4—5.
There are five bees.

Skip Counting

You can count past 9.
You can count 10—11—12—13—14—15.
To count faster, you can **skip count**.
Instead of counting one at a time, you can
count by twos: 2—4—6—8—10,
count by threes: 3—6—9—12,
or count by fives: 5—10—15—20.
You can skip count by any number you want!

Skip count by threes. How many frogs do you see?

The 9 frogs in the water plus this frog make 10 frogs. Turn the page to see why ten is special.

After Ten

You use the **digits** 0 through 9 to write numbers.

Any number more than 9 needs more than one digit. After 9 comes 10, then 11. Ten is the first number that has two digits.

Count the leaves. Ten is a full set of numbers!

For the number of leaves on this tree, you would need many digits!

Counting Teens

The numbers 11 through 19 are the **teens**. The teens each have two digits. Each number from 11 to 19 is a set of 10 with a number left over.

eleven 11 one full set of ten and one left over

twelve 12 one full set of ten and two left over

thirteen 13 one full set of ten and three left over

fourteen 14 one full set of ten and four left over

fifteen 15 one full set of ten and five left over

sixteen 16 one full set of ten and six left over

seventeen 17 one full set of ten and seven left over

eighteen 18 one full set of ten and eight left over

nineteen 19 one full set of ten and nine left over

This pond can hold one set of 10 ducks.	
How many sets of 10 are in the pond?	1
How many ducks are left over?	3
How many ducks in total?	13

Larger Numbers

The last teen number is 19. What number is next? That is right, 20. The number 20 is made up of two full sets of 10.

Think of the number 21. This number is made up of two full sets of 10. The 1 tells you that there is one left over.

Each leaf can hold one set of 10 ants.	
How many leaves are there?	2
How many ants are left over?	1
How many ants in total?	21

You can count flowers in a field.
You can count all kinds of things!

Tens and Ones

Here are three blankets with bunnies. There are others bunnies nearby. There are ten bunnies on each blanket. Any bunnies off the blankets are left over.

Full sets are also called "tens." Left overs are called "ones." Count the bunnies using sets of tens and ones.

Tens	3
Ones	2
Total	32

Greater Numbers

Look at the pictures. Decide which
number of crabs is greater. How?
You can count. Counting is easy
with numbers less than 10.

Look at the rocks and the beach.
Which place has more crabs? Which
number is bigger? The place that has
more crabs has the greater number
of crabs.

Activity Box

Try drawing 10 crabs on a boat.
Draw 5 crabs left over, in the water.

How many crabs are
there all together?

Comparing Tens

Look at the numbers 34 and 41. **Compare** them. What numbers are in the tens places? You are right: 3 and 4!

Is 3 or 4 bigger? That's right: 4. So 41 is bigger than 34. It does not matter what number of ones are left over. Four tens are more than three tens. You do not need to count if you compare tens.

Activity Box

You can write **>** instead of **greater than**. You can write **<** instead of **less than**. On paper, write 34 < 41. Then turn it around 41 > 34.

34

What symbol would you use here?
34 ___ 41

41

Number Order

Here are three numbers: 9, 17, 12.

Look at the tens place. Is one number larger in the tens place? If so, that number is bigger. If the tens are the same, look at the ones. That will tell which is bigger or smaller. Finding **order** is like a game!

	Tens	Ones	Total
Duck	0	9	9
Bird	1	7	17
Bunny	1	2	12

Activity Box

Place 9, 17, and 12 in number order. Go from smallest to largest.

Glossary

compare To see what is the same or different

digit A number symbol

greater than >; more than another amount

less than <; fewer than another amount

order To list more than two numbers from least to greatest

skip count To count by numbers other than 1

teen A number from 11 to 19

zero	0		eleven	11
one	1		twelve	12
two	2		thirteen	13
three	3		fourteen	14
four	4		fifteen	15
five	5		sixteen	16
six	6		seventeen	17
seven	7		eighteen	18
eight	8		nineteen	19
nine	9		twenty	20
ten	10			

Index

Printed in the U.S.A. — CG